THE ULTIMATE BUG OUT BAG FOR PETS
EVACUATING WITH PETS, SHORT-TERM AND ZOMBIE APOCALYPSE!

BY J. GODSEY

SICPRESS 2012
METHUEN, MA

Thank you to Dr. Kim Trahan-McFarland and the crew at Animal Rescue Veterinary Clinic, the volunteers at Animal Rescue Merrimack Valley and my friends, human, wolf hybrid and otherwise at the Wolf Adventure.

©*J. Godsey/Sicpress.com 2012*
Methuen, MA.

Table of Contents

Why prepare an evacuation kit? 5

Where are you evacuating to? 7

What should you bring with you? 10

Emergency Information 13

First Aid Kit 17

Bug out Bag Contents for Dogs 22

Checklist for a Dog Bug out Bag 28

Bug out Bag for a Cat 29

Checklist for a Cat Bug out Bag 35

Bug Out Bags for Other Pets 36

Additional Resources 40

Author Info 41

WHY PREPARE AN EVACUATION KIT?

Bugging out - To the 'prepper' and survivalist communities, it means getting out on your own, believing that leaving your home is necessary for your immediate survival.

Zombie apocalypses not withstanding, weather emergencies such as hurricanes, ice storms, tornados and flooding and their attendant power outages, are causing the displacement of entire neighborhoods with increasing frequency. Hazardous material spills can happen anytime along any highway or rail line. Utility service networks are no longer local and are increasingly becoming more interconnected regionally; this leads to outages that knock out wider areas of the country. Information disconnects between government and non-government agencies and insurance companies can make it difficult to return to damaged homes quickly.

When and if it happens, we hope leaving our home in an emergency will be only temporary. Regardless of the reason, one is evacuating or 'bugging out', never leave your pets behind. The rule of thumb is: "If it isn't safe for you, it isn't safe for your pets." They usually do not survive on their own, and you cannot count on coming back to get or tend to them later. Pets left to fend for themselves are likely to become victims of exposure, starvation, predators, contaminated food or water, or accidents. Leaving dogs tied or chained outside in a disaster is a death sentence. One should take appropriate steps to care for them during this transition, just as you would do in your home.

The likelihood of you and your pets surviving a emergency such as a fire, flood, tornado or terrorist attack depends largely on the planning you do ahead of time. Before Hurricane Katrina demonstrated otherwise, Americans as a whole considered being prepared for an immediate evacuation at all times to be something other people did; people who lived in zones prone to earthquakes, wild fires or floods. What we have seen is that it can happen to anyone, anytime and without warning. Even our own community's emergency resources may itself be compromised by an unexpected event. Preparation for unforeseen events is a responsible act, which at the very least, puts a part of our mind at ease knowing we have done what we can ahead of time.

Leaving your home with your pets can be a planned and organized event, such as when one has lost power and have no heat due to an ice storm, or rapidly when the water if rising faster than you can pack. If you think you may be gone for only a day, assume that you may not be allowed to return for several weeks. It is hoped that some preplanning can help one decide what our priorities are in the moment or give us comfort that we have a support system in place.

This guide is compiled from interviews with people who have had first hand practical experience with evacuation, local veterinarians, animal control officers, and materials such as those provided by the Federal Emergency Management Administration, Massachusetts Emergency Management Administration, the Humane Society of the United States and the American Veterinary Medical Association. By writing this, I hope to inspire the reader to plan their pet's fate with the same care and foresight as they would for their human family.

Where are you evacuating to?

Evacuate early - Don't wait for a mandatory evacuation, people who have to be evacuated by emergency personnel have been told to leave their pets behind. Evacuating before conditions become severe will keep everyone safer and make the process less stressful

Only a small percentage of evacuees go to shelters, the majority end up with relatives, friends, and hotels. Some states have mandates that evacuation shelters must make provision for pets, as yet some shelters do not. Many hotels are not pet friendly. Many of us have well-meaning friends and relations whose homes are not pet friendly. If you have pets with you, then you need to decide in advance which arrangements which are the most appropriate. If you have your pet's evacuation kit at hand, it will make the transition less of a hardship.

If you choose a location that is inside your immediate area, you may have to choose a secondary location outside of your area, because if your have lost power, your local friends and relatives may have as well.

Shelters - The major part of preparation is doing your research, do not wait until disaster strikes to make your plans. Search your state and local communities emergency management website for information about pet shelter care before deciding where to go in an emergency plans. Local and state health and safety regulations do not permit the Red Cross to allow pets in Red Cross disaster shelters. Call your city hall's emergency management director and ask them well ahead of an emergency occasion. The Pets Evacuation and Transportation Standards Act (PETS Act) of 2006 requires local and state emergency preparedness authorities to include in their evacuation plans how they will accommodate household pets and service animals in the event of a major disaster. Local and state authorities must submit these plans in order to qualify for grants from the Federal Emergency Management Agency (FEMA). In some areas, regional and local animal rescue agencies will set up separate facilities for animal sheltering depending on how severe the emergency. In some communities, the human evacuation shelter is within the same room, facility, or campus as accommodations for pets. This allows the animals' owners to have a large role in caring for the pet. In other communities, the human shelter and pet shelter may be in separate locations. In this case, evacuees are told where to bring their pets, while they will be staying at a shelter for people. (Rabies certificates mandatory for any shelter.)

Hotels - If you can afford it, hotels are great short-term relocation solution for your family. You needn't worry about keeping your family safe and together in a shelter, and you have access to food, communications, electricity and plumbing. More hotels are becoming pet friendly, some hotels that required a non-refundable deposit but the cost is well worth the peace of mind. If you wish to leave your hotel room without your dog/cat, many hotels require that the animal be kenneled. This is as much for your pet's protection as it is for the establishment, you don't want the staff opening the door and letting your pet escape, especially if they don't know it is inside.

Find out which ones are in your evacuation zones, while you still have access to the internet. (Rabies certificates necessary for hotels and motels and other public accommodations.) Here are some websites to help you find one in and out of your relocation area:

Bringfido.com, Dogfriendly.com, Doginmysuitcase.com, GoPetFriendly.com, Pet-friendly-hotels.net, Pets-allowed-hotels.com, Petswelcome.com, Tripswithpets.com.

Friends and relatives - If you expect to go to the home of a relative, even if your relative is accepting, theirs may not be a pet friendly home. You have to bring everything you need with you to make as little impact on their lifestyle. If this is your most secure and likely bug out location, it may work out well to leave the large part of your pet's bug out bag there.

Boarding - Another option is to arrange a caretaker for your pet in case of emergency. If you and your family are located in a non-pet shelter or hotel, your pet can be boarded or cared for by a friend or professional. (Rabies certificates mandatory for professional boarding services.)

Buddy system - If there is an emergency at your home and you are not there, the best solution is a pet care buddy: someone with whom you can reciprocate pet emergency evacuation duties. This is a person to whom you are entrusting the care of your pet in the event that something should happen to you. A friend or neighbor, who has keys to your home, knows your pet, and where your pet's bug out bag is located. Pre-arrange a meet up location inside your immediate area and one outside of your immediate area, in case communications aren't possible. It is suggested that you sign a letter releasing your neighbor of liability in case your animals become injured or escape, as well as signing a veterinary medical treatment authorization for treatment form.

What should you bring with you?

Ready made emergency kits for people and pets are available all over the internet from nearly every large vendor or specialty supplier. Some have been put together with care and planning, but others not all. Usually assembled by persons just guessing what someone in your position may need. You should not rely solely on a preassembled kit to completely cater to the specific needs of your and your pet.

Always customize any emergency kit by adding and removing items appropriately. Personally assembled kits are more efficient and useful, than ones assembled by strangers in a one-size-fits-all form. With customization, you know what you have, and you know how to use it and what else you need.

Ideally the 'ultimate bug out bag' is one that includes everything you may need to maintain your pet in another location or in transit with no loss of quality of life for either of you. If you don't have something in your own personal emergency supplies, you can usually make do, borrow or do without, if you are missing something that your pet needs, there may not be a suitable substitute available when you most need it. If you have the time and opportunity to put the best pet emergency evacuation kit together then "it is better to have it and not need it, than need it and not have it."

Types of supplies

Information - The more information about you and your pet, that you have at hand the easier transitions will be.

Food - Nearly all emergency references advise at least three days of food and water, some even advise one or two weeks of food, water and bedding. Obviously, it all depends on your location, the types of disasters you are fleeing from and immediately and likely availability of the supplies your pet requires. If you are in a wild fire zone where if you flee it will probably be for good, more is always better than less.

Containment - Having enough carriers to transport all your pets can make the difference between its life and death. The worst thing imaginable is to remove your pet from its comfort zone and then it gets lost in an unknown location. Don't trust cats. Cats should be contained when transported and once it gets to the evacuation location. Small dogs the same for the most part, except when carried. Medium to large dogs may have to be contained when you personally aren't on the other end of their leash. When your pet is securely contained, it is safe from getting lost in the confusion or perhaps injuring someone or getting injured themselves.

Exercise - Leashes, leads, tie out cables, even secure ropes, whatever you need to securely control your. Even with small dogs and cats, leashes attached to harnesses will ensure the animal stays connected to you when it is not contained.

Sanitation - Food goes in one end, something else comes out the other, and usually at inopportune times. Evacuations are a stressful time and dog digestive systems are especially susceptible to stress. Cats are more subscript with their personal evacuations, but can practically vomit on command and are very disseminating with their cat litter. You need to be prepared to clean up after your pet, even their odor can make your pet very unpopular in a public situation.

Medical care - Obviously, you will need duplicates of all your pet's everyday medications, as well as those only taken infrequently. You never know when you will have to evacuate, and it is usually at the most inconvenient time. You should also bring whatever pet first aid supplies (which are surprisingly similar to human first aid supplies,) you feel comfortable administering. Having extra supplies with you allows someone else the chance to use them for your pet's comfort or someone else's pet's comfort.

Kit Container - Nearly everything except large volumes of food will fit into a decent size gate-mouth canvas tool bag or a small rolling carry on. Plastic lidded bins are not necessarily convenient for transport, the lids do not always stay closed, and they take two hands to carry. Even a small pet kennel makes a better storage and transport container than one that requires two hands. A backpack seems like an obvious option, but that should be reserved for human emergency supplies. Once loaded, your bug out bag can be stored next to, on top or even inside your pet's cage or carrier. You only have to remember to rotate any food or treats stored inside.

Emergency Information

Regardless of whether you are evacuating, digging in or not even in an emergency situation at all, gathering and organizing all of your pet's information for quick reference is an essential part of responsible pet ownership.

Emergency Contact Data - Make a list of contact information for your nearest relations, your pet care buddy, your regular veterinarian, your emergency veterinarian, local animal control, area animal rescue groups, humane societies, and SPCAs. Hopefully, most of this information will not be needed, but should you need additional assistance, finding these numbers quickly without the internet is difficult.

Medical/Vaccination Records - Whenever you visit the veterinarian, you should have your pet's records in hand. Assemble your pet's medical records in a stack, with the oldest ones at the bottom and the newest on the top. Scan them in that order; and then staple them together. If your pile is too big to staple together, do it in sections. But don't worry, this step just makes paging through them easier for people looking for some particular piece of data, as it allows one to see the history of the pet chronologically with the most recent vaccines on the top.

Those paper folders with check boxes for vaccinations are not medical records, these are only reminders for you. Vaccination and treatment records have the names of the drugs and vaccines with the dates and amounts given and the veterinarian's name.

Rabies Certificate - Surprisingly, rabies tags on collars aren't valid 'documents'; an actual piece of paper, a rabies 'certificate' is what you need. Although the tag can be accepted to allow your pet entrance into shelter situations. Having your pet's rabies vaccine updated on a regular basis is a must if your pet spends any time with other pets, at a dog park, a groomer, a boarding facility. Without a current rabies certificate, you may possible be excluded from hotels, shelters, and other public accommodations.

Inserted microchip - Micro-chipping pets is becoming increasingly more popular. If you have adopted your pet from a shelter, or purchased it from a breeder, the odds are good your pet already has a microchip. If it does not, contact your veterinarian about inserting one. They cost very little, and there is usually a small service charge to register it. Some companies require a yearly charge to allow you to change the information in the future.

There are three or four major companies that sell and service microchips. The good thing is that if you call HomeAgain.com with a 24PetWatch.com number, they will tell you that it is the number from a different company and give you the correct 800 number.

If your pet has a chip number on their medical records and you don't know where it is registered you can use PetMicroChipLookup.org to figure it out.

You can register your pet's number with more than one company. If your pet is still registered to a previous owner you can usually just call and change the data without much hassle.

Recent Photographs - A must have for identifying your pet. Even if you have checked your pet into a shelter or boarding facility, temporary collars and internal identification systems aren't infallible, two golden retrievers look similar to someone who doesn't know any better.

Most pets don't change their appearance drastically during their life. If yours does, then multiple images are handy, perhaps before and after grooming. Take the time to find a decent image which shows relative height and weight, and markings. It helps if you are in the picture, then there is no question about ownership. Printed copies should be attached to the medical records and digital versions created as well.

Proof of Ownership - Medical records and photographs usually do the trick, but if you have license, registration, proof of purchase or any other paper work include a copy in your packet. The best proof of ownership is always a photo of you with your pet.

Digital Files - Put both the medical records and the images on a flash drive, it will be a very, very small amount of data so it will fit on the smallest one you have lying around. This drive should be kept in your evacuation kit, or duplicated and attached to your pet's collar and in your wallet, even in your phone, or other cloud storage. Keep in mind that in an emergency situation, internet and computer access probably won't be available and your paper copy rabies certificate is the difference between checking into a shelter or a hotel and not. The digital file is a back up in case a copy needs to be printed or sent to another location, it saves the step of scanning.

Waterproof Pouch - Store all the paperwork and photos inside a clear plastic folder, one that secures closed, a plastic zippered pouch is ideal. Waterproofing isn't just for water, this packet sometimes ends up in the bag with the food and water and other sticky materials.

In case of an emergency clothes-on-your-back-only evacuation, a copy of your pet's medical records are what you grab; perhaps even keeping this pouch in your personal bug out bag or any place equally convenient. If you don't have the paper records, then the flash drive is the next best thing.

Cloud and internet storage of the records is useful, but at times of crisis, the power and internet are among the first things to go.

When you are not home

Aside from your Buddy System buddy, rescue personnel and animal control may arrive at your home before you and should be given all the help possible to try to rescue your pets.

Window Decals - Obtain 'Pets Inside' sticker and place them on your doors and windows. The ASPCA offers them for free. Label them with the number and type of pets in your home, also add a contact number here you can be reached in case of emergency. When evacuating, try to remember to write the words 'Evacuated with Pets' across the sticker or elsewhere on your front door. [http://www.aspca.org/about-us/free-aspca-stuff/free-pet-safety-pack.aspx]

Other information for rescue personnel you can add to this sticker or another prominent place near your front door, would be location of rescue supplies. Among the rescue supplies, should be cages, carriers, muzzles, handling gloves, and catch nets, so that strangers can try to rescue your pets with the best chance of keeping everyone unharmed.

Include a contact number for the Buddy system buddy as well as your regular veterinarian and/or boarding facility.

First Aid Kit

In an emergency where your pet has already been injured, your task is to get it stabilized and transport it to a veterinarian. This is not the time to start learning pet first aid. If your dog is in pain, it may not understand you are trying to help it, and it may bite you, making it a much worse situation than just leaving your dog alone until you can get it to a professional. If you have some experience with treating your pet, then pack what you feel comfortable with using. But having extra supplies with you allows someone else the chance to use them for your pet's comfort or someone else's pet's comfort.

Talk to your vet - When you have a chance have this conversation with your veterinarian. Explain that you are putting together a disaster kit because you want access to prescription items before your pet is actually ill. Items such as a bag of fluids, tubing and needles, which are relatively shelf stable, and are essential in helping a severely dehydrated or malnourish animal, you need to get from your vet.

First Aid Kit - Red Cross First Aid kit is well priced and comes in a convenient fanny pack. You can start with any ready-made pet first aid kit and then revamp it to suit your needs, or just put your own together from scratch, sometimes for less money if you take a turn through the dollar store.   [http://www.redcrossstore.org/Shopper/Product.aspx?UniqueItemId=613]

    o **Pet First Aid Guide** - The Red Cross has a suitable title: Pet First Aid: Cats & Dogs, indeed you could choose any book or guide from any reputable source. Give it a good thumb through when not under the stress of an emergency, at the very least it will give you something to read while waiting around at your evacuation location. [http://www.amazon.com/Pet-First-Aid-Cats-Dogs/dp/157857000X/]

o **Pouch** - Any sturdy plain bright red zippered pouch, like a travel, shaving or toiletry kit makes a good container.

o **Scissors** - Inexpensive utility bandage scissors, cheap light with the safety tips, they can be found at dollar stores now.

o **Bandages** - standard roll gauze bandages, gauze squares, self adherent bandage.

o **Tape** - Water proof first aid tape, but the traditional white stuff is fine.

o **Pen Light** - this is surprisingly helpful, when you need to do things like look in an ear, or check to see if a bone is stuck. Don't settle for the cheapest on the market, not the most expensive; for any emergency kit tools, you want sturdy dependable but something you will regret losing. Dorcy is known for good LED flashlights and don't forget the batteries.

o **Emergency Blanket** - Made of the silvery mylar that reflects body heat inward. Any brand will do, you buy a pack of ten for ten dollars and divvy them up between family members and pets.

o **Instant Heat pack** - The small hand warming or even the larger ones; these can be placed inside a carrier or cage under the towel to bring the temp up.

o **Instant Cold Pack** - The cheapish disposable kind, just like in humans good for sprains, and muscle injuries etc.

o **Nytrile Gloves** - Or Latex. The Nytrile are synthetic latex and purple. You only need a couple of pairs, you should be able the get fresh pairs donated by your vet or doctor. Store them in a ziplock bag inside the kit.

o **Tongue depressors** - These have 1001 uses, scooping pet food, blending medicines and combining the two. Also useful for dislodging sticks from between dog teeth.

o **Topical antibiotic** - Neosporin type triple antibiotic ointment. Provides a great protection for hot spots or cuts and punctures to prevent infections.

o **Isopropyl Alcohol** - Quick disinfection of nearly everything.

o **Hydrogen Peroxide** - Pain free, disinfecting wounds and scratches

o **Saline Solution** - In a squirt bottle, used for irrigating wounds and washing out eyes and ears.

o **Petroleum Jelly.** Whether used as a lubricant for thermometers or used to protect from frostbite, only a small tube or container is needed.

o **Digital Pet Thermometer** - If a digital thermometer is in your everyday pet first aid kit, a duplicate in your bug out bag would not go amiss. Normal temp for both dogs and cats is $100º-102.5º$. The thermometer should be almost clean when removed. Any sign of blood, diarrhea, or black, tarry stools should be checked by a veterinarian.

o **Tweezers** - Even if they are only useful for pulling fleas and ticks, then these have done their job. If you scout around, especially in the dollar stores, you can find large sized ones that you can get a grip on.

o **Magnifier** - You just need something inexpensive, preferably plastic that you can use to get a closer look down an ear or at a wound or mostly for reading labels. The best cheapest place to find these is the drugstore, down by the prescription counter.

o **Needle-nose pliers** - A cheap pair has many uses beyond porcupines quills & thorns. Safely removing a stubborn can lid is one.

o **Chemical Light sticks** - Same as with a human emergency kit, cold instant light is always welcome. An inexpensive box of ten eight-hour sticks can be divided between human and pet kits.

o **Flash Light** - You can never have too many. Battery operated flashlights need batteries, crank dynamo LED flash lights don't need batteries. Either one is essential for any evacuation kit. Finding your pet in the dark is only one use. A hands free headlamp is ideal.

o **Pet Nail Clippers** - The type with good handles for gripping or even large human toe nail clippers in a pinch, you can clip more than just nails with these, like fishing line and hooks.

o **A broad spectrum antibiotic** - a 'just in case' prescription medication. Pets can pick up things under stress that they wouldn't normally. If you settle into your new location and you suddenly have a leaky nose or eyes, it is "better to have and not need than need and not have." **Doxycycline** is a member of the tetracycline antibiotics group, and is commonly used to treat a variety of infections. Doxy does not need refrigeration and will keep in storage. (needs a prescription) o **Canned Pumpkin** - The fiber in the pumpkin helps fight diarrhea and upset stomach, canned pumpkin can keep practically forever and can be mixed with their food.

o **Instant Oatmeal** - When mixed with your pets food this will help absorb the extra fluids in an upset stomach and help combat diarrhea easily.

BUG OUT BAG CONTENTS FOR DOGS

Duplicate Collar with ID Tag - Your dog should already be wearing a collar with identity, rabies, and microchip tags. 'Just in case' it gets lost or detached, having a duplicate handy can't hurt.

Slip lead - Slip leads just slip over the dogs head to work, the tighter they pull the tighter it gets. It is the standard dog handling lead used by professionals. It is easier to slip the loop over the head of a nervous dog than it is to fumble around trying to find the D ring to attach a clip to it.

Towel or Blanket - An obvious mainstay for any dog, a little smell of bedding from home. A towel can always be used for what towels do best.

Folding Crate - For transport and safe containment where you get where you are going you need a container large enough for your pet to turn around and lie down, perhaps even eat. If your dog does not have a crate for everyday use, a collapsible one for emergencies is a good idea. Some pet friendly shelters have cages, but some may not. If you end up in the home of a relative or friend without much space, your pet will be happier with his own space. MidwestPetProducts.com seems to be the dominant supplier in the field, with good quality cages.

Pet Carrier - Smallish and toy dogs should have hard sided carriers, they feel less vulnerable in a crowded area. The soft collapsible carriers may be lightweight to carry, but are not very good otherwise and it is too easy to trip over and squish the occupant. Avoid carriers with plastic doors, the carrier can stretch and the doors pop open. Petmate Vari-Kennel can be stacked and are pretty indestructible. Nylabone makes a fold flat pet carrier with a metal door, if you nearly never need a carrier for your dog, this may be the one to put in your emergency kit.

Food Dishes - The type that screw or hang onto the cage/carrier make less mess, but they are problematic if you are breaking down and setting up the cage in a short amount of time. A couple of nesting stainless bowls for dry food and water, work fine. Disposable plates and bowls are more common in shelter use, especially for wet food.

Food and Water - Put aside at least three days worth of your dog's regular food for portability. Some organizations advise keeping as much as two weeks worth of food, which would be ideal for a long displacement, but unwieldy. Perhaps storing more food at your evacuation location would be practical. Rotate this stored food once year to keep it fresh. A 5 gallon water bottle is common and convenient or a weeks worth of water for people and pets. Manual Vacuum pumps are available to allow easy tapping without the bother of a gravity feed system.

Five year shelf life emergency pre-packed food is available. It should be treated as back up food for your back up food. If you can avoid it, don't try feeding your pet a new brand of food in a stressful environment, they may get irritable bowel or an upset stomach if they eat it, or they may just turn their nose up at it.

- Can opener - If you are feeding wet food, indeed they all have pull rings now, but if the ring snaps off you will be grateful for a $5 manual can opener. For my money there is no other brand than Swing-a-way. I have tried flimsy no brand can openers and have had them bend while in use. A GI P-38 Can Opener is a great survival tool, but it can just as easily cause an injury, if you find yourself fumble with wet fingers and a sharp lid.

- Pet food can cover - These are worth their weight in gold. There isn't really a decent substitution for them. Can covers are very cheap and universal. Keep a couple in the bag in case one gets dropped and rolls away.

- Treats and Chew toys - You will need bribes and distractions. Whether it is moving your pet in and out of the carriers and crates or distracting them from the noise and commotion.

- Toys - If you haven't brought their favorite toy, at least stash a duplicate in the emergency gear. Combating stress is important, an unhappy or frightened dog can get sick or dangerous.

- Muzzle - An appropriate sized Quick Fit style nylon fabric muzzle for your dog. These are put on the dog from behind the head and cinched quickly, before they have a chance to use their paw to remove it. It helps to have someone else holding the dog appropriately: with one arm up around the chest and another around the neck pressing the dog to themselves. Muzzles should only be used for short times such as nail trimming and injections and then removed, as long it is safe to do so. If the dog is upset, wait for the dog to calm down before removing it. These are NOT used to quiet a barking dog, that's where the treats, chew toys and bribery comes in. [http://www.fourpaws.com/products/quick-fit-muzzle.htm]

Prescriptions and Heartworm Medications - If your dog is on heartworm medication or any other regularly taken medication, keep at least one dose in your evacuation kit. You can't control when you will be asked to leave your home, but it will always be at the most inconvenient time.

Flea and Tick Medication - One dose of a topical back of the neck, flea and tick product, Advantix or Frontline. Your pet may not have them now, but when you come home in three days, you don't want any surprises.

Canned Pumpkin - One can to combat irritable bowel should it arise. Do YOU want to be the one with the dog with diarrhea? Yogurt helps with too, but a can of pumpkin keeps longer. (for can opener see above)

Cleaning products and paper towels - You don't know how valuable paper towels are until you don't have them. Paper napkins grabbed off the coffee table don't work after the first few seconds of getting wet. A roll of paper towels and a disinfecting spray can take care of accidents and all the abutting surfaces. This especially matters, if you and your pets are imposing on a friend or relation's home.

Trash bags - For scooping poop, recycled shopping bags work well for everyday yse, but they need to be undamaged or they will leak. In an evacuation situation, that is an extra frustration you don't need. One small roll of waste bags stowed in your kit takes up very little room and solves the problem. A large kitchen trash bag or two will be handy to put your single bags into as well as waste cleanup materials. It is impolite to put little bags of poop into human waste receptacles without warning.

Water Purification Tables - These don't cost much, but in flood zones, clean water may be hard to come by and extra bottled water may be scarce. Adding it to your pet's water may save you problems down the road. Potable aqua tablets should be in the human emergency kit anyway.

Bleach - A small container of bleach could come in handy as common bleach has many uses, most commonly bleaching things. As a disinfectant it should be diluted nine parts water to one part bleach. When used to purify water, use 8 drops for a gallon of water, stir well and let stand for at least 30 minutes before use.

Collapsible Water Carrier - Depending on where you live and what you are being evacuated from, it is also helpful for using the purification tables. These may already be in your personal kit. A 1 or 2 gallon Fold A Jug or other collapsible bladder, takes up much less room than an empty milk jug, and is relatively cheap.

Rope Line and Anchor - Just because your dog comes when you call it, doesn't mean other folks want him sniffing their pant leg. With a 15 foot tie out cable and a ground stake you can put your dog out in your relatives back yard without causing much fuss.

Saddle Bag - If your dog is large enough to carry a saddlebag, he probably can, working will keep him distracted and busy as well as help you with the chores. Get him used to a saddle-bag before hand, an emergency is not the time to introduce it. Don't put the first aid kit or the medical records in the pack in case it gets wet or you get separated from your dog. The new Outward Hound bags come in a variety of colors and sizes. [myoutwardhound.com]

Car Window Pet Gate - These are a relatively new product, but may be well worth the effort if you may be traveling or leaving your dog in the car during the warm season. These expandable car window pet gates, are designed to provide a screened air flow area between the window and the car door frame. [http://www.amazon.com/Pet-Parade-Car-Window-Gate/dp/B007II01D8]

Checklist for a Dog Bug out Bag

- ☐ Kit Container
- ☐ Microchip
- ☐ Collar w/ID Tag
- ☐ Records Pouch
- ☐ Photographs
- ☐ Medical/Vaccination Records
- ☐ Rabies Certificate
- ☐ Flash Drive w/ Digital Files
- ☐ Slip Lead
- ☐ Large towel or blanket
- ☐ Folding Crate
- ☐ Pet Carrier
- ☐ Food Dishes
- ☐ Food
- ☐ Water
- ☐ Can opener
- ☐ Can cover
- ☐ Pumpkin
- ☐ Treats / Chew toys
- ☐ Toy
- ☐ Muzzle
- ☐ Trash bags
- ☐ Disinfectant Spray bottle
- ☐ Paper towels
- ☐ First Aid Kit
- ☐ Prescriptions
- ☐ Heartworm Medications
- ☐ Flea and Tick Medication
- ☐ Water Purification Tablets
- ☐ Chemical Light sticks
- ☐ Collapsible Water Carrier
- ☐ Rope Line and Anchor
- ☐ Saddle Bag
- ☐ Flash Light

BUG OUT BAG FOR A CAT

Duplicate Collar with ID Tag - Your cat may not wear a collar normally but 'Just in case' it gets separated from you or out of its cage, it should be wearing one. Recent studies have shown that the old fashioned 'non break away' type are no more dangerous than the breakaway style; and in this particular short term situation, you certainly don't want the collar with ID to break away.

Harness with leash - Unless you do it on a regular basis 'walking' your cat is a drag, literally. If you have to take them out of the container, it is best that they are attached to you. There are short leash with harness sets or you can use a retractable leash. If they take off and you let go of the handle, it whips behind them and they stop and stare at it, giving you the chance to grab it.

Towel - A towel or two are always welcome additions; whether inside the carrier or cage for bedding, draped around the cage as a calming influence or wrapped around the cat for restraint.

Cat Carrier - The soft collapsible carriers may be lightweight to carry, but are not very good for habitation and it is too easy to trip over and squish the occupant. You can get away with smallish carriers for just transport and use a folding cage later or use a very large kennel that will double as a cage when you get where you're going. If your cat doesn't travel much at all, it may develop a fear of the carrier. Leaving the carrier in the living room open with blankets and toys inside, turns something to fear, into a personal cat cave. Petmate's Veri Kennel can be stacked and are pretty indestructible. Nylabone makes a fold flat pet carrier with a metal door, if you live in a small home or apartment, this is a great solid carrier.

Folding cage - Cats don't enjoy travel, so it is going to stay contained as much as possible, along with the litter box, food dishes, and bedding. If you end up in the home of a relative or friend without much space, your cat will be happier in its own space. Small kennels will not hold much than a cat and a towel, but most folding cages have enough room for a litter pan and food dishes. The type with the side door are immensely valuable since you can put the cages in multiple locations. A good sized towel or small blanket can come in handy to partially cover the cage to lower the stress level. If the cage is medium to large, you can put the entire cat carrier inside the cage, and your cat can use the carrier like a cave to hide in. Midwest Life seems to be the dominant supplier in the field.

Don't store folding cages outside or where the will get rusty, it makes them difficult to collapse. And it shows disrespect for your pets. You can wrap them in trash bags or tarps, but the moisture may still get in.

Food dishes - Cats make a project out of spilling their water bowls. If you can get them, choose ones that hang on the side like stainless steel cage cups, or anti splash water bowl. Some of the food dishes for bird cages work just as well for cats.

Food and water - Put aside at least three days worth of your cats regular food. Rotate it in storage to keep it fresh. Three days is the standard for emergency rations, but you have to allow for spillage and spoilage.

Your cat may decided he doesn't like being caged and toss all the food on the ground. If you have to move to a new location after you have put out food, you may have to chuck it and start again later. Cats like dogs don't need to have wet food all the time, it may be less messy to switch to dry for the duration of the displacement. Avoid using the five year shelf life pet food unless you have run out of options, your cat is finicky in the best of times.

Can opener - If you are feeding wet food, indeed they all have pull rings now, but if the ring snaps off you will be grateful for a $5 manual can opener. For my money there is no other brand than Swing-a-way. I have tried flimsy no brand can openers and have had them bend while in use. A GI P-38 Can Opener is a great survival tool, but it can just as easily cause an injury, if you find yourself fumble with wet fingers and a sharp lid.

Pet food can cover - These are worth their weight in gold. There isn't really a decent substitution for them. Can covers are very cheap and universal. Keep a couple handy in case one gets dropped and rolls away.

Treats - Bribes are handy to keep them distracted while you change their litter or dishes.

Prescriptions Medications - If your cat is on any regularly taken medication, keep at least one dose in your evacuation kit. You can't control when you will be asked to leave your home, but it will always be at the most inconvenient time.

Flea and Tick Medication - One dose of a topical back of the neck product, Advantage or Revolution. Your pet may not have them now, but when you come home in three days, you don't want any surprises.

Cat Muzzle - The Quick Fit nylon fabric type, which fits over their face and eyes, very useful for nail clipping and quick vaccinations of a stressed out cat. A cat's head isn't the only end to watch out for, when working with a uncooperative patient, scruffing at the neck is vital. Other resources advising carrying a cat like a football, this puts the back claws in close proximity to your midsection. First wrap the cat's body and legs in a towel, then it can be carried safely. Ideally, they shouldn't be carried that far at all, once you are finished working with them put them back in their carrier or cage, still wrapped in the towel is safest.

Toys - Cats can make a toy out of anything, crumpled paper, milk jug cap rings, the cheapest toy mouse or crinkly toy in the carrier may give you something to interact with them. Catnip is ideal for a calming influence in a stressful situation.

Litter and litter boxes - Which type you use depends on whether you are heading to a short-term temporary location or a long term temporary location. If you are leaving your home to a secondary location, a small cat litter pan and a container of litter would be appropriate, even better if you have already stocked that location. But generally, if you are unsure of where you will end up or you may have to move an already loaded litter pan. In a pinch, you can use aluminum baking pans, or small boxes cut down, and fill them with woodstove pellets, shredded newspaper, papertowels, even leaves all easily disposed of after use. Cat's Pride makes an already loaded disposable litter tray, that peels open like a tv-dinner. [http://www.catspride.com/]

Litter scoop - Even if you are using clay non-scoopable litter, keeping it as clean as possible makes it last longer and smell better. You will notice is that your cat will spend a lot of time lounging in a clean litter box, if they are suddenly not in it, then it is time to scoop it.

Cleaning products and paper towels - You don't know how valuable paper towels are until you don't have them. Paper napkins grabbed off the coffee table don't work after the first few seconds of getting wet. A roll of paper towels and a disinfecting spray can take care of accidents and all the abutting surfaces. This especially makes a difference, if you and your pets are imposing on a friend or relation's home.

Water Purification Tables - These don't cost much, but in flood zones, clean water may be hard to come by and extra bottled water may be scarce. Adding it to your pet's water may save you problems down the road. Potable aqua tablets should be in the human emergency kit anyway.

Bleach. A small container of bleach could come in handy as common bleach has many uses, most commonly bleaching things. As a disinfectant it should be diluted nine parts water to one part bleach. When used to purify water, use 8 drops for a gallon of water, stir well and let stand for at least 30 minutes before use.

Collapsible Water Carrier - Depending on where you live and what you are being evacuated from, it is also helpful for using the purification tables. These may already be in your personal kit. A 1 or 2 gallon Fold A Jug or other collapsible bladder, takes up much less room than an empty milk jug, and is relatively cheap.

Trash bags - You will need extra little bags to scoop litter into, as well as take your cleaning debris. Recycled shopping bags work well, but they need to be undamaged, litter gets everywhere and clay litter mixed with water makes floor slick. You also may be putting cat feces into receptacles for human trash and it should stay contained. Transporting open litter pans with litter makes a mess. If you need to move your litter pan, unload it into a trash bag and then reload it with the same litter when you get where you're going.

What to do if your cat gets loose.

If accidents happen and your cat gets loose in a contained area, a net can be helpful to retrieve it from under wherever it is hiding. In a shelter situation with pet accommodations, there will be professionals around with the proper skills and equipment to help retrieve your cat safely.

However if you are in a location where YOU are the professional you need to recover your cat with the least amount of chaos and stress. Once you have your cat cornered, let it calm down. Talk softly to it and try not to approach it from the front. If you can approach it from above or behind, scruff it quickly and strongly pressing it against the surface until you can gain control. Ideally you should be able to lift it up and grab its back feet and put it back in the carrier quickly. DO NOT LET GO until the animal is back in its carrier or cage.

When trying to load an uncooperative cat into a carrier, turn the carrier upside down like a trash can, and lower the cat from above, so it enters the cage feet first, then close the gate quickly.

Folding Net - This is not an expensive net designed to entangle an animal. Sneak the net toward the animal from the side or back, where it can't see you, use it as you would a towel: to compress the cat against a surface so you can scruff it. Scruff it through the net, wrap it in a towel and put it back in its cage. Frabill Capture Nets [http://frabill.com/landing-nets/capture-nets.html]

Checklist for a Cat Bug out Bag

- ☐ Evacuation Kit Container
- ☐ Microchip
- ☐ Collar with ID Tag
- ☐ Records Pouch
- ☐ Photographs
- ☐ Medical/Vaccination Records
- ☐ Rabies Certificate
- ☐ Flash Drive with Digital Files
- ☐ Harness with leash
- ☐ Cat Carrier
- ☐ Folding cage
- ☐ Towels
- ☐ Food dishes
- ☐ Food
- ☐ Water
- ☐ Can opener
- ☐ Pet food can covers
- ☐ Treats
- ☐ Toys
- ☐ Litter
- ☐ Litter boxes
- ☐ Litter scoop
- ☐ Trash bags
- ☐ Disinfectant Spray
- ☐ Household Bleach
- ☐ Paper towels
- ☐ First Aid Kit
- ☐ Cat Muzzle
- ☐ Prescriptions
- ☐ Flea and Tick Medication
- ☐ Water Purification Tablets
- ☐ Chemical Light sticks
- ☐ Collapsible Water Carrier
- ☐ Folding Net
- ☐ Flash Light

Bug Out Bags for Other Pets

Like Dogs and Cats, other house pets small or large require the same supplies to continue their care away from home: Containment, sanitation, food and water, and first aid and medical care. But each species requires its specific needs catered to even more so than with dogs and cats. You REALLY won't be able to count on finding those supplies in an emergency situation.

> **Folding Net** - If accidents happen and your pet gets loose in a contained area, this can be helpful to retrieve it from under wherever it is hiding. Once you have your pet cornered, let it calm down, you can use the net as you would a towel to compress it against a surface so you can collect it, of if you have a larger capture net you can entangle it, but remember it will not appreciate it. Gloves are recommended.   (Frabill Folding Net with Telescoping handle / Frabill Capture Net)

First Aid Kit

Disinfectant Spray bottle

Paper towels

Trash bags

Extra instant heating or cold packs if necessary.

Water Purification Tablets

Collapsible Water Carrier

> A **Plastic Watering Can** such as one would use to water houseplants, can be used to add seeds, food, and water into cages without opening the doors.

Bugging out with Birds

Proof of ownership if possible

Recent photos

Leg Bands for identification

Food and water for a week or more

Fruits and vegetables for extra hydration

Vitamin and nutritional supplements to combat stress.

Carrier. Birds should always transported in a travel carrier, not overly large for its size.

Extra newspapers for lining the carrier.

Larger towel or blanket to cover the cage not just for cold weather, this also helps reduce stress when traveling. For warm weather, a bed sheet will work in a pinch to keep them calm without overheating.

A spray bottle to periodically moisten your bird's feathers, in hot weather.

Kwik stop styptic powder

A timed pet feeder, will insure that your birds eat on schedule.

Proper habitation cage for your evacuation location.

Toys and distractions

Capture net appropriate to your bird's size, with a long handle

Handling gloves if appropriate

Bugging out with Reptiles

Proof of ownership if possible

Recent photos

Food and water for a week, preferably frozen or dried not live food. Insects and such shouldn't be introduced into a shelter or public accommodation environment; it will make you very unpopular.

Vitamin and nutritional supplements to combat stress.

Carrier. Snakes may be transported in pillowcases, but permanent and secure housing will be needed when you get to your evacuation location, such as plastic containers with secure locking lids.

A sturdy bowl that is large for your pet to soak in.

Heating pad or other warming device, such as a hot water bottle or instant heat packs. Large lizards can be transported in carriers like birds, instant heat packs can be added to the carriers for transport.

Bugging out with other Small Animals: Rabbits, Chinchillas, Hamsters, gerbils, mice and guinea pigs, etc.

Carrier. Very secure carriers suitable for habitation when you get where you're going. Avoid moving small animals from container to container, that's when escapes occur. Ideally, you should pick up their container and take it with you whole.

First Aid Kit, reduced to suit their needs.

Food bowls

Water bottle, with an extra, just in case.

Food and water and bedding for a week.

Salt lick, nutritional supplements

Small hidebox or card board tubes.

Instant cold packs, Rabbits and Guinea Pigs can overheat easily.

Additional Resources

Federal Emergency Management Association (FEMA): Caring for animals in an Emergency. http://www.ready.gov/animals

Downloadable FEMA: Pet Owners Brochure. http://www.ready.gov/sites/default/files/documents/files/pets_brochure.pdf

American Veterinary Association publication for disaster preparedness: Saving the Whole Family. https://ebusiness.avma.org/EBusiness50/ProductCatalog/product.aspx?ID=140

Humane Society of the US: Make a Disaster Plan for Pets. http://www.humanesociety.org/issues/animal_rescue/tips/pets-disaster.html

American Society for the Prevention of Cruelty to Animals: (ASPCA Disaster Preparedness) http://www.aspca.org/pet-care/disaster-preparedness

Red Cross Disaster Preparedness: Pet Safety http://www.redcross.org/prepare/disaster/pet-safety

Author Info

J. Godsey, is a publisher, editor and ghost writer with Sicpress.com. She has been doing voluntary pet and wildlife rescue for over 12 years; as well as working with Animal Rescue Merrimack Valley in Massachusetts and Animal Rescue Veterinary Services of Londonderry, NH, and Wolf Adventure wildlife rescue and rehabilitation of Goffstown, NH. She has brought her experience with animal handling to her community's Community Emergency Response Team.

Please review this book online.

If you have any suggestions for inclusion please contact sales@sicpress.com

Your purchase goes towards animal rescue care and rehabilitation.

www.ingramcontent.com/pod-product-compliance
Lightning Source LLC
Chambersburg PA
CBHW071314060426
42444CB00034B/2592